Doubting Thomas's Book of Common Prayers

poems by

Thomas Burton

Finishing Line Press
Georgetown, Kentucky

Doubting Thomas's Book of Common Prayers

Editor: Christen Kincaid

Cover Photo: Benjamin Alexander Dugger, The Thomas Window in stained
glass, Seeger Memorial Chapel, Milligan College

Author Photo: Jim Sledge, ETSU Photographic Services

Cover Design: Elizabeth Maines

Printed in the USA on acid-free paper.
Order online: www.finishinglinepress.com
              also available on amazon.com

Author inquiries and mail orders:
Finishing Line Press
P. O. Box 1626
Georgetown, Kentucky 40324
U. S. A.

Contents

Preface

Human limitation coupled with apparent abandonment has not been more dramatically expressed than by the words: "My God, my God, why hast thou forsaken me?"

But the feeling is common to most of us. Frustrations with self, with personal beliefs, with relationships human and spiritual, with the nature of things—all seem like Samuel Johnson's apprehensions, beasts we never slay, only continually beat back to their dens. Even poets seem to have no adequate response. Their bootless cries, as well as ours, often "trouble deaf heaven" with "no language but a cry," even though they—as we must—challenge monsters of the dark and deep with heroic fortitude in overcoming doubt and despair.

Some of these common frustrations without the security of a net or golden chain from heaven are the inspiration of these spiritual, non-religious prayers.

I am indebted to the readings of the poems by friends and colleagues, as well as their encouragement, especially Carolyn Wilson, David Hatcher, Ben Dugger, Jesse Graves, and Rolly Harwell.

On Being a Little Angry

Lord, I am a little angry.
Maybe I've got the crazies as well.
I'm really not angry just with you,
but kind of mad at everything:
The world's going its way presumptuously
and seemingly owes me nothing.
So to hell with it—isn't that what you say?
What I need is vision.
I'm down here mucking around
and don't know what in hell I'm doing.
By the way, I don't buy your zapping Uzzah
for trying to hold the ark, the dumb ox stumbling.

On There Being No One Else

Lord, you don't talk to me,
but since there's no one else to tell my feelings to,
I'll talk up to you.
No need to mince my words as with humans
unless you're a Setebos to my Caliban.
If you were human—
even if you were one of the few who are in tune with what I say—
and you and I were exploring the mixing of our atoms or anatomies,
we would be on guard lest the need of accepting reality exceeded
    capabilities,
and we would note only harmonies, not cacophonies.
We wouldn't want to know what's out of joint, just dovetails in—
not where scratches were, but consummate smoothness.
Who wants to hear, "Here you miss, or there exceed the mark"?
With humans your thoughts must be parceled out: lovers, this;
    friends, that; associates and strangers, the rest—
sometimes "I must hold my tongue" and other times "whipt for
    holding my peace."
Come to think, though, you're not deaf to critique yourself;
but, as is written, on the mount took "Horeble" exception.

On Someone to Work Things Out

Lord, I understand why people believe in you,
having someone directing things toward good
regardless of how they appeared.
It would be great to have someone say,
"That's okay that you failed—you did the best you could—
I'll take over now and make it right.
And all the muck in your life won't matter
in the one that is to follow."
God! I want all things to "work together for good,"
or at least okay.
And to believe in one who could work it out would be good,
great if someone did.

On When There's Nobody

Lord, David had to be a stand-up kind of guy.
Yet when he was down-and-out and needed a little help,
he often went to you.
And there were times when he went to others too, like Bathsheba.
Guess he didn't feel you were enough—he needed flesh and blood
(although, as heroes are wont, he probably thought he shouldn't
    have).
And you should've felt no jealousy since you had made him that way.
But what did David do when he didn't have Bathsheba,
a man who shouldn't show the chinks in his armor?
And what about anybody when there's nobody,
but who needs somebody?
Let's face it, a god's a little abstract.
I look unto the hills, and I only see a lot of trees.

On Dealing with Reality

Lord, why do two people get angry and turn away from each other?
When things aren't right is the time they need the other the most, to
    say the least.
You should certainly know a lot about that.
You had one of the best in heaven say, "To hell with it all" and then
    run out on you.
The story goes you threw him out, but I believe it wasn't that way.
I think he rebelled and got out of there, not because you forced
    him out
and not because you were intolerable and not because things were
    so bad—
I think he got mad and opposed you because the truth was too hard
    for him to face.
He couldn't cope with it, so he flew the coop.
It was too much for him to reveal the truth and say to you:
        This isn't all it was planned to be.
        Our spirits aren't fusing, this isn't doing it for me.
        I think I'm changing even if you're not.
        It's hardly heavenly bliss, I'm miserable as hell.
        I'm one way, it seems, and you're another.
        I'm not fitting in here anymore, let's fix it or quit.
        I'm not blaming you—maybe it's just your nature—
        and for heaven's sake you shouldn't blame me for mine.
        But I'm not alone in this, others feel the same as I.
        If we can't work it out, I'll make it somewhere else.
        There are other spheres, you know.
        And if I cannot "make a heaven of hell,"
        with some help from you, deservedly,
        I can make something better than this
        with all chaos breaking loose.
But he didn't—that would've taken some stooping.
Yet had he been able to deal with reality—

even if you hadn't been perfect, and he certainly wasn't—
there would have been no war in heaven.
Perhaps his nature had absorbed too much of darkness
to deal with that much light, so he obfuscated it:

> I'm tired of being kicked in the teeth
> [the head or however the text goes].
> I'm tired of always being second,
> I ain't gonna be treated this a-way.
> You might enjoy playing god, but not me.
> You've even gone out and got someone to take my place.
> Now, by damn, you'll pay for it, I'm going to give you hell.

That's, no doubt, when he caused all that trouble and went away
    mad—
making you look pretty bad too.
Of course he sweated for it.
But if he once loved you and you were good and he were good,
you should have worked out something for good—
at least for better than all that worse, all that hurt and suffering.
Why can't two humans do that, why can't they deal with reality?
Are they too demonic?

On Disunity

Lord, how do you cope with a dearly beloved
who's more and more, less one with you?
How long do you share whatever's left over and overlook the rest?
What's your point of no return, "This far and no more"?
I know your flaming sword has cut off quite a few,
yet the son of man seems longer-suff'ring than you.
How much then should we sustain?
To hang on more, we could care less;
for caring too much—like your son—we're pulled out of joint.

On the Cruelest Month

"April is the cruelest month"?—Eliot, no!
Rather this one with grayness everywhere.
For now there is a strange, pungent smoke
diffusing about the temple that's a holy place to me.

On Fixing It

Lord, I don't like what's going on—so fix it.
I can't or I would.
For the love of god, do it if you can.
I don't know if I can stand anymore.
Maybe this is just another reality I'm supposed to face;
but I don't care, I'm coming apart at the seams.
Damn it, do something good for pity's sake— that's supposedly
    your job.

On the Roughest Day

Lord, I know that "come what come may,"
you say there's a season for everything.
What's this one for—to pluck up, cast away, rail against, run to,
strike back, tear down, turn from, weep for, wade on, or keep silent?
I guess the time is to love "through the roughest day" and look to the
    morrow.

On Giving Up the Faith

Lord, I know at times you overlook a failure in deed,
even ent'ring Astarte's tent, by one after your own heart.
But what about when one gives up the faith
and treads underfoot the pearl?

On Detachment

Lord, I know there is a time to keep and a time to cast away,
a time for jessing a hawk to nurture it
and a time for loosing it "to prey at fortune."
A time to quit deep feelings of "despised love,"
which murder sleep that knits up the golden, airy thread unraveling.
A time to relinquish longing for another, who's shuffling off to be
     free
and whose closeness lessens, ipso facto.
Yet detachment seems like giving up.
Or is choice that which freedom is all about, the sine qua non?

On Rocky Ground

Why so steep and rocky, Lord?
Sorry, I don't accept that tale of garden
cankered with Adam's blowing it
and his seed's growing among the weeds.
Why not fertile soil, bathed by sweet-showering skies?
Self-pitying question, no doubt,
since I stand not on sterile ground.
But why such wind and rain—
the nature of things, you say, rose and briar?
I should be glad of a daisy touched, though plucked from reach?
Has all the field been gleaned with night coming on,
and this shade, a shadow of the final swath
which cuts machination short?—
all mysteries requiring the wisdom of a Solomon,
my having known a lily of the field.

On Waste

Haven't talked to you in some time, Lord.
My transmission power went down in solitude.
But now I must say, I could have used a little help,
a jump start at least.
I might also add there's a lot of waste in what I've been through.
All that stuff I learned through the years—what programs to watch,
which flowers to buy, when to order anchovies,
where to store the picnic basket, how much cream in the coffee—
completely useless now.
I suppose it's best to just forget all that—if I could.

On the Creative Force

I'm told the creative force of *something* from *nothing* was love divine.
Seems to me that human love is much the same:
it creates that which exists as long as certain criteria persist.
Love, like a seedling too dry, may die,
but nurtured. grow into a towering strength.
Even "the ax laid unto the root" and fruitless hewn down,
Love once created, like a child who dies, still lives in memory.
Lord, can you uncreate something into nothing?
I can't.

On Being Alone

Everyone's coming to you saying,
"Save me, Jesus; heal me, Lord; help me carry my load."
But "whom seek ye" when it's lonely as a tomb
after they've come and gone?
Guess you just go on alone
because that goes with the territory.

On Stimulation of Consciousness

Lord, I need something to stimulate my consciousness,
to wake me out of my sleep, my drowsy existence—
a book, a poem, a song, a conversation.
Your silence makes my talking to you seem senseless.
If there were anybody else, I wouldn't bother you.
But I need someone to think with.
Ideas bounce around the walls of my head
like a racket ball or a hammer on a blacksmith's anvil.
And even if I forge a thought,
I can't tell if it rings true unless I sound it out.
I just can't seem to reason in isolation.
Talking with someone, though,
I can slice off a thought and see if I can swallow it.
Guess I'm using you like certain friends:
I lay all my cards on the table,
and it's all right whether or not they pick any up.
But there's a difference.
Those friends have a certain slant of mind
and know what I'm talking about—and generally respond.
With you, everything has to be assumed,
and I wonder if you're like someone else I knew
whom I considered more than friend, "one another's best,"
who empathized with my every thought—
my god, was I ever wrong!
But really, I don't have a clue about you.

On Mucking Through

Lord, it seems like living is just mucking through.
We can't fulfill or be fulfilled,
we can't escape the hurting or being hurt—
imperfection to the core.
Some, like you, create their own world,
with a pantheon of golden idols and Elysian Fields.
It gives them means to make it—what else's a heaven for?
Maybe just mucking through the best we can is good enough,
better than freezing up or melting into a dew.

On the Groaning Spirit

Does my spirit groan, Lord, because *yours* did
    when you breathed into us the breath of life?
    Must life begin and end this way?
    Is your spirit within evoking the desire
    to be more than we can be:
    ever more understanding, more creative, more in control?
    Is your spirit simply more willing than our weakly flesh?
    How much groaning will take off the edge?
Or does the *human* spirit
    (which makes us more than dog or rat)
    see with godlike vision how limited we are
    and provoke our groans by misinterpreting human requisites?
    Whereas living—caring, trying, breathing deep and into
        others—
    after all, is enough?

On Opening Up

Since I haven't been talking much with you,
I've tried to talk with others—
 "Open up," they say, "it helps a lot."
But if I talk with "know-it-alls," I resent what they say.
If simply "rubber stamps," it doesn't help.
If "brick walls," it's frustrating.
If sensual, sensitive females, I quickly get in over my head.
And if I track the caverns of my mind to their "inmost cell,"
it's much too much to ask anyone else to follow.
Truth is, generally no one really cares that much,
so I'm right back where I started—solo.
Then there's you, Lord.
Are you listening empathically,
or am I whistling in the wind?

On the Holy Grail

Lord, there's much about the knights of the Grail I envy.
They were skilled and thoroughly fit.
Some, better than others, but all of the very best,
bound together by faith and high calling—
unimaginable to ride with Perceval seeking the ideal!
But most important to me is the affirmation:
giving up would have been disgraceful,
but those who fulfilled the quest would know
"Our faith was true and we failed not."
It's not the same for you to hold out a carrot,
a heaven somewhere out there in the future.
If I made it to heaven, I wouldn't need confirmation.
It's now I need the Grail.

On Being World Class

Lord, I'd like to be world-class in something.
I'm not sure it would matter so much in what.
It wouldn't have to be the best of anything,
but world-class in something.
Intellect would be nice, or artistry.
Samson was in strength; Solomon, wisdom; and David, heart.
For pity's sake, I'd take any one of the three.
How about as mentor, lover, or friend?
You've surely done more for less deserving—
I know, also less for more talented—
but I feel I would make us both proud.
I'd be no Achilles in his tent—sorry, no Elijah oblivious of his
      peers—
and if you wanted to go big time,
you could put me in the class of Michael the Archangel.
Not even Lucifer could withstand him.
How about my being a world-class human Michael?
But anyone who says "You can be anything you want to be"
is full of *teufelsdrockh*.
Approach the figure of Michael, who is like unto God?
who intuits the mind of God? leads the seraphim?
and wields that terrible swift sword?
No way—the only chance I see is to be a world-class human.
No Michael, but still mind boggling.

On a Disease

Lord, recently I visited Jeanie.
Her body swung around like an Appalachian Limber Jack
to a wild, cacophonous tune unheard by me.
"Parkinson's—it's a sorry disease," she said;
"it doesn't give you a chance."
Should I be angry at you for her or grateful for me?
Neither she nor I deserve what we have.
Deserve, I guess, is really neither here nor there,
but mostly we feel we should get what we deserve,
that is, escape the whipping.
A lot of those who deem themselves your children
would have the rest of us believe they're like special plants
in some mighty, green-thumbed gardener's hothouse.
I think we're rather like the seeds that fall
random along the wayside or on fertile ground.
Marcus Aurelius makes a lot of sense:
what happens is all in the nature of things—
neither good nor bad, but simply *is*.
Jesus posed about the same thing, wouldn't you agree?

> Think ye that the Siloam men crushed by a tower
> were offenders above all those that dwell in Jerusalem?
> I tell you, Nay.

I'd go along with that.
Still, a sorry disease—Marcus and Jesus notwithstanding.

On a Heaven

Lord, I wish there were indeed a heaven.
There are so many I'd like to tell some things that never got said.
There was Jo Ann in the third grade.
> She's the one who won me over from the blonde-haired girl
> who jumped on my back.
> I painted JAM, her initials, on the stern of my battery-
> powered motorboat.
> I only hope she knows that when we went to the afternoon
> movie—
> which my grandmother didn't approve of on Sunday—
> she didn't have to place the dime admission in my hand
> on the way down the aisle.
> (Come to think, since then I've always paid when I've gone
> down the aisle.)
And that summer I stayed with my country kin, working in the wheat.
> What a harvest!
> The box supper seemed innocuous enough, and would have
> been,
> if I hadn't gotten the help of one cousin in bidding against
> another one
> for his girl's prize basket.
> A few hours eating and one in the cool of the following
> evening,
> when she brought some homemade ice cream over after I'd
> worked all day,
> lost her perhaps a suitor and me might near a cousin.
> In a couple of days, however, I was back in the city,
> and I never had a clue if she knew what it meant
> for her to have given out the basket's description over the
> eight-party line,
> or what those days mean to me.

And there was Cathy, the older of two sisters who lived over near the
canal.
   She used to get cramps in her legs, and she would rub them
      with Sea Breeze
   while mine set up with rigor mortis.
   Lord, your anointing with oil can't hold a candle to that.
   I remember dancing with her in the gym one time when it
      was hot,
   and she kept wiping the perspiration unmercifully from her
      upper lip.
   She didn't seem overly interested in me,
   and later on I dated her sister, who was also pretty,
   but had no muscle contractions.
   I never had the courage to ask if I could massage those legs,
   but if Cathy and I make it to a heaven, I hope you have some
      Sea Breeze.
There was that girl, younger than I, who went to the state meet,
   I think, just to see me perform.
   God, what provocative lips.
   I did get to kiss them a few times, but not to tell her
   "A thing of beauty is a joy forever."
   I moved away after that, and she disappeared I know not
      where.
And there was another girl way back in sixth grade at the class pool
party.
   The teacher—the one who sent me to the office
   because her dress got caught accidentally on my crossed foot
   as she was passing down the row—
   kicked both the girl and me out of the pool for kissing under
      water.
   So we went down to the ocean where Neptune didn't seem to
      mind.

I saw her years after when she was selling jewelry in a store,
and I wanted to tell her then, I'd never forget our baptism.
She was the sixth grade's Sophia Loren with the same
features—
really out of my class, but she surely inspired my seeing
lots of Italian movies.
Speaking of movies: Romy Schneider was in the first art film I ever
saw.
I was in college— she on the screen in a little theater in
Nashville.
I don't know if you like art films or not, you may prefer Cecil
B. De Mille.
Anyway, her husband, I think, had mistreated her in some
way.
She, despondent, was disrobing in a luscious bathroom,
and suddenly I knew the difference between aesthetic and
erotic.
The luxury of Romy's bath contributed, I'm sure,
but only a part to the consummate beauty of the scene.
I used to think that painters were simply crazed with sex,
but once I saw a living Renoir, I began to understand
a poet's marveling: "Two hundred years to adore each
breast"—
absolute beauty, idea stamped on space, overwhelming,
the best thing, perhaps, you've ever created, yummy as well.
Would Romy, I wonder, in heaven be interested in my
response?
Or would I have to have been a movie star as well?
It took me a long time to be conscious of a lot of this sort of thing.
In Tennyson's "Oenone," for example, why would Paris run
off
and leave his lovely nymph for Aphrodite's promise of Helen,
the fairest loving wife in Greece?

Then one day I was studying the poem in a class with Rita,
a queen of beauty if ever there was one; and I knew,
though I never really knew Rita.
I didn't get to tell her she was the best critique of a poem I
    ever saw.
"Age cannot wither her, nor custom stale her infinite
    variety"—
and for that Antony willingly traded Rome.
Oh yes, there's also Jack's neighbor,
        whom I met when I stayed overnight in his house at end of
        term.
        I never had the chance to respond to what she said
        after the movie and smooching in the car parked under
        Spanish moss—
        on her back porch, the curfew met and the last time I'd ever
        see her—
        the final words from her foam-born form:
        "Thank you for not taking advantage of me tonight."
Who knows what if things had been in sync
and I'd had a chance to have my say?
Who knows where the wind blows?

On Human Contact

It's human contact I want, human contact.
Some mutual recognition with another person
that both are simply trying to make it through.
Dispense with competition, acquisition, all that other stuff,
and confirm we're not aliens very strange on this planet,
just strangers very alienated.
Don't people know their tickets, tourist or first class, are restricted?
They're flying high and low or taxiing on the ground a limited time?
Then their baggage's unloaded, their tickets voided?

On Breaking the Hedge

Lord, shouldn't people know our appreciation?
But when the person's the opposite sex,
the "hedge" can be broken and the serpent bite.
Intimacy with his "little pin bores" in,
and farewell castle wall.
No harm in human spirits touching others,
creating new realms.
But those nouveau states have few restrictions,
and the wall torn down
reveals what the court inside requires,
what everybody needs—the realization of the soul.
"The sting's in that."
Since your Spirit supposedly "moved upon the face" of the deep,
it should know, only too well, that the waters can get muddy,
and if you don't want to swim, you'd better not get wet.

On Commitment

Lord, I don't know what all I do believe,
but I know I'm part of more than comprehended.
Who knows, maybe that "more" is you.
Also, I'm not sure how I fit into it all,
but here I am with limited brain and feelings,
with the sense that I'm to make the best of it.
Yet to make it at all, I'll have to commit to something,
and commitment in fact may be belief.
Now's the time, not as some tragic hero
to sit upon the ground and mourn all the might-have-beens,
soiled plumes, and "milk of human kindness" spilt—
but as some epic hero
to lay on till damned Despair itself cries out, "'Hold, enough.'"

On Being Out of the Ashes

Lately, Lord, I haven't needed to talk to you—
I'm no longer smothered in ashes,
flame licked, with no breath to nourish the coals.
Now I have a commitment
and feel ignited, alive, burning.
Yet, always feel free to call on me.
And if need be, I'll call on you.

Thomas Burton, Professor Emeritus of English (East Tennessee State University), is the author/editor of three monographs and six books, including four published by the University of Tennessee Press. His work has focused on Appalachian culture and ranges from traditional balladry to religious serpent handling. He has done considerable fieldwork on Scottish Travellers, produced documentary films, and published poetry and fiction. His highly allusive narrative entitled *Michael and the War in Heaven* is forthcoming from the Overmountain Press, and his poetry is represented in *The Southern Poetry Anthology*, vol. 6, *Tennessee*.

A native Tennessean, he received the B.A. degree from David Lipscomb University and the M.A. and Ph.D. degrees from Vanderbilt University. He founded and directed the ETSU Appalachian-Scottish Studies Program, was president of the Tennessee Philological Association and the Tennessee Folklore Society. He is the author of scholarly papers and created four major collections in the ETSU Archives of Appalachia. Awards include the Appalachian Consortium Laurel Leaves Award, the E.T.S.U. College of Arts and Sciences Award in Teaching, the Best Documentary (Sinking Creek Film Festival), the Sycamore Shoals Celtic Festival Heritage Award, and the Friends of the Johnson City Public Library Achievement Award.

Burton is the father of four sons and resides in Johnson City, Tennessee, where he continues writing at home and at East Tennessee State University.

www.ingramcontent.com/pod-product-compliance
Lightning Source LLC
LaVergne TN
LVHW091234080426
835509LV00009B/1271